The Lucky Litter:

Wolf Pups Rescued from Wildfire

by Jennifer Keats Curtis

photography by John Gomes

Through the hazy smoke, the tired firefighter raced up the hill on his all-terrain vehicle (ATV). He stopped to secure his gear and looked down . . . what was that little black ball of fluff? A bear? No, that was definitely a tail.

The creature looked up. Her blue eyes locked with the firefighter's blue eyes: a wolf pup. So young. What was she doing out of her den? The firefighter called for help.

Help came in the form of a wildlife biologist who examined the den—a deep hole below a hollow tree. There were no tracks, which meant no adult wolves were caring for the babies. The biologist tried to climb in. He was too tall. A smaller firefighter scrambled into the lair. One by one, he pulled out the litter—two grey, three black.

The small, fuzzy babies wobbled rather than walked, but their eyes were open. They were probably three weeks old.

The firefighters named the two girls and two of the boys after their villages: Gannett, Huslia, Hooper, and Stebbins. The last boy, X-Ray, they named for their firefighting team.

The fluffy pups were covered in dirt and something worse—porcupine quills. They clearly needed help.

First, medics made sure the babies got a drink through a plastic tube and plunger called a syringe. Then, the pups were flown to the Alaska Zoo.

At the animal hospital, vets and keepers rushed into action. After the pups weighed in at less than three pounds, it was chow time.

The hungry pups drank special milk out of a bottle. To keep away infection, the vets removed the porcupine quills and gave the pups medicine to keep them healthy.

Then, the vets checked their sharp milk teeth, which were just starting to come in.

After a quick toenail clipping, the vets examined the babies' blue eyes.

Over the next few weeks, the eyes would turn brown and then the golden yellow of an adult.

Like most babies, Gannett, Hooper, Huslia, Stebbins, and X-Ray were only awake long enough to eat.

They fell asleep by themselves. They slept in a heap as if they were still in their den.

In time, the wolves moved to an outside enclosure, near another pack of wolves: six adult brothers and sisters. Although the pups could not touch the other wolves, they were close enough to see, smell, and definitely hear the adults. Sometimes the zoo was very noisy. When the big wolves howled, the little ones joined right in.

Because the wolves were so young, they needed lots of attention. The keepers often had to hold several at a time.

Like other animal babies, Gannett, Hooper, Huslia, Stebbins, and X-Ray explored. And they played.

They played with each other. They played with toys, and they chomped on them.

Hooper loved to gnaw on Kong® dog toys.

Gannett was fond of sticks.

Hooper and Huslia liked stuffed animals.
So did X-Ray.

The pups chased each other around the tree . . .

. . . and around each other.

Gannett liked to play hide and seek.

Under the care of the keepers and vets, the pack grew quickly.

Baby fuzz began falling out. Adult hair grew in.

As they grew older, the litter began acting more like adult wolves. Wolves live in packs. They play together, hunt together, and sleep together. But all packs have a leader and rankings. That means each wolf has a place in the pack.

Wild wolves hunt moose, deer, elk, and other animals. The adults bring food back for the youngsters. In the zoo, the keepers put meat into their bowls. At first, the pack ate together. But as they matured, they began growling over their food.

During play, some of the pups fought over the toys. Others would drop down meekly. Gannett and X-Ray became the pack leaders (alphas).

By the time the pups were nine weeks old, they weighed between 12 and 15 pounds and were very healthy. It was time for them to move to their permanent home at the Minnesota Zoo.

When the pack arrived, they spent a short time in quarantine, away from all of the other animals at the zoo so that the keepers could be sure they were healthy. Then, the lucky litter moved to a special wolf exhibit. There, they could smell and hear, but not touch the other animals, including lynx, porcupines, beavers, black bears, a wolverine, and a coyote.

At the Minnesota Zoo, the wolves roam happily. They chomp on antlers, sniff special scents that keepers spray for them, and play with Boomer Balls.

With zookeepers and vets caring for them, the pack of five will remain together for life.

Stebbins

Huslia

Hooper

Gannett

X-Ray

For Creative Minds

Wildlife Rescue Sequencing

Put the wildlife rescue events in order to spell the scrambled word.

L Once the animals have seen a veterinarian, they need a safe, quiet space to rest and recover. Places like zoos and rehabilitation centers care for the animals. Keepers and rehabilitators nurse the animals and provide for their basic needs until they are better.

F After the animals are fully recovered, they need a place to live. Many are released back into the wild. Some animals have become reliant on humans, never learned how to live in the wild, or need lifelong care. These animals find a permanent home in a zoo, wildlife sanctuary, or education center.

O After sick or injured animals are brought in from the wild, the first focus is helping them feel better. A veterinarian will treat them, just like a doctor treats human patients. The animals might need medicine or even surgery.

W Even wild animals can be injured, sick, or orphaned. If you ever find any injured wild animals, do not approach them. They don't know that you want to help and may try to defend themselves. Sometimes the parents are out finding food and will come right back. Call a wildlife professional, who can take these animals to a place they can get help if they need it.

Answer: WOLF

Growing Bodies

All animals change as they grow. Some newborn animals, like wolves, have a different eye color than they will have as adults. A newborn's soft fur or hair changes color or texture. As animals get older, their bodies change shape. They get taller. They gain weight. Some animals are born with large heads or paws. As they grow, these body parts shrink in proportion to the rest of their bodies. How else can bodies change as animals grow?

Look at the pictures below. How does Gannett's body change as she grows from a newborn into an adult? What traits stay the same? How can you tell this is the same wolf?

How has your body changed since you were little? If you look at pictures of yourself from when you were younger, what has stayed the same? What is different? If you could see a picture of yourself ten years in the future, do you think you would recognize yourself?

Keystone Species: Wolves

A keystone is the big, important stone at the top of an arch. It holds all of the other stones in place. The keystone anchors the structure so that it does not collapse.

Keystone species are animals that help all of the other animals in an ecosystem stay in place. An ecosystem is made of all the living things (like plants and animals) and non-living things (like water and earth) in an area. All of the parts of an ecosystem are connected to each other. If something happens to a plant or animal in that ecosystem, the whole system could be affected. If something happens to a keystone species, the whole system could even collapse.

The gray wolf is a keystone species. Gray wolves may be small in number but they play a large role from the top of the food chain all the way to the bottom. They help keep the balance between predator and prey.

Scientific Observation:
Gray Wolves in Yellowstone National Park

When a keystone species is harmed, the entire ecosystem suffers. Scientists were able to observe this effect when the gray wolves disappeared from Yellowstone National Park. In the 19th century, people did not know that wolves were a keystone species. People hunted gray wolves until there were none left in Yellowstone. Without any wolves, the elk population boomed. All of those elk needed to eat. They ate so many plants that there wasn't enough food for all of them. The elk became sick and they starved. Because the elk ate so much, many trees could not grow. Without big trees, beavers were affected and there was less shade over the river. Many fish left the area. The absence of the wolves affected not just the elk, but also the plants, the beavers, the river, the fish—the entire ecosystem.

In 1995, scientists reintroduced gray wolves to Yellowstone. With plenty of elk to eat, the wolves flourished and so did the rest of the ecosystem. Coyotes, eagles, and other wildlife scavenged the remains of the elk killed by the wolves. Trees and shrubs could grow since the elk had not eaten all of them. Bears ate the berries that grew on shrubs. Trees grew taller and gave shade to the river. Beavers thrived and fish returned.

The return of the gray wolf to Yellowstone National Park helped bring balance back to the animals and plants of the park.

Wildfire

Some wildfires start naturally, usually after a lightning strike. But the majority of wildfires are caused by people. The wildfire in this story was started by humans in 2014. It burned along the Funny River in Kenai National Wildlife Refuge in Alaska. The Funny River Fire burned 105 square miles (272 square kilometers) of forest and left a litter of young wolves without an adult pack to care for them.

You can help prevent unwanted wildfires. Pay attention to fire warnings. Never leave a burning campfire unattended and make sure to completely put out your campfire before you leave. It can quickly catch and spread out of control. Don't litter. Some types of litter (like matches or cigarettes) can start fires and other litter can provide fuel for a growing wildfire.

Once a wildfire starts, firefighters have to decide if they need to put it out, contain it, or let it burn. This is not always an easy decision.

Wildfires can help the forest. Wildfires burn away dead trees, dry leaves, and other plant matter. This helps clear out old plants to make room for new growth. Some plants, like lodgepole pines, need wildfires in order for their cones to open and grow new trees.

But wildfires can also hurt the forest. They drive animals (including humans) out of their homes. Animals can be killed, injured, or orphaned by a wildfire. When wildfires grow too hot, they can consume healthy plants. Instead of just clearing out old plant matter, strong wildfires can burn entire forests to the ground.

Fire needs fuel to burn. A firebreak is a place where there are no plants or other material for the fire to burn. Roads make good firebreaks. Sometimes a very strong wind can blow the flames and ash across the firebreak. But usually when a wildfire reaches the firebreak, it cannot cross over to the other side.

For Kym Kilbourne and Kelly Brown, my beloved pack members—JKC

For their input, photographs, and fabulous details about the fire, the rescue, and the animals, many thanks to:

· Sean Corrigan, Assistant Fire Chief with the Seward Volunteer Fire Department
· Leah Eskelin, Kenai National Wildlife Refuge Park Ranger
· Mark Fletcher, Yukon firefighter
· Nadia Ham, photographer
· Pat Lampi and Shannon Jensen from the Alaska Zoo
· Kelly Lessard, Tom Ness, Josh Le, Delaina Clemetson, Chris Forslin, Ashley Ondricek, and Galen Sjostrom from the Minnesota Zoo
· Sue Mann, Designed by Sioux
· Jeff Selinger, Wildlife Biologist, Alaska Department of Fish and Game

Firefighter Mark Fletcher with Ganne

Library of Congress Cataloging-in-Publication Data

Curtis, Jennifer Keats, author.
  The lucky litter : wolf pups rescued from wildfire / by Jennifer Keats Curtis ; photography by John Gomes.
    pages cm
  Audience: 4-8.
  Includes bibliographical references.
  ISBN 978-1-62855-718-3 (english hardcover) -- ISBN 978-1-62855-719-0 (english pbk.) -- ISBN 978-1-62855-721-3 (english downloadable ebook) -- ISBN 978-1-62855-723-7 (english interactive dual-language ebook) -- ISBN 978-1-62855-720-6 (spanish pbk.) -- ISBN (invalid) 978-1-62855-722-0 (spanish downloadable ebook) -- ISBN 978-1-62855-724-4 (spanish interactive dual-language ebook) 1. Wolves--Infancy--Juvenile literature. Zoo animals--Infancy--Juvenile literature. 3. Animal rescue--Juvenile literature. 4. Wildfires--Juvenile literature. I. Gomes, John (John G.), illustrator. II. Title.
  QL737.C22C87 2015
  599.773'139--dc23
                              2015018904

Translated into Spanish: La camada con suerte: cachorros de lobo rescatados de un incendio forestal

key phrases for educators: EE (Environmental Education), changing habitats, keystone species, natural disasters (wildfire), wildlife rehabilitation, zoos

Bibliography:
"Gray Wolf (Canis Lupus)." USFWS: Q and A's about Gray Wolf Biology. N.p., n.d. Web.
Green, Emily. Wolves. Minneapolis: Bellwether Media, 2011. By Emily K. Green. Web.
"How Wolves Change Rivers." How Wolves Change Rivers by Sustainable Human. YouTube, 13 Feb. 2014. Web
"Inside a Wolf Den." YouTube. YouTube, n.d. Web.
"International Wolf Center." International Wolf Center RSS. N.p., n.d. Web.
McLeese, Don. Gray Wolves. Vero Beach, FL: Rourke Pub., 2011. Print.
"Photos: Residents Evacuated as Funny River Fire Rapidly Grows in Size." Alaska Dispatch. Alaska Dispatch, n. Web.
"Rain Falls on Funny River Fire, Provides Some Relief." KTOO. N.p., n.d. Web.
"Wolves, Wolf Pictures, Wolf Facts - National Geographic." National Geographic. N.p., n.d. Web.
"Yukon Man Discovers Den of Wolf Pups Near Edge of Alaska Wildfire." The Prince George Citizen. Canadian Press, 30 May 2014. Web.

Manufactured in China, June 201
This product conforms to CPSIA 200
First Printir

Arbordale Publishir
Mt. Pleasant, SC 2946
www.ArbordalePublishing.co